MONSTROUS MANNERS

MANNERS AT A RESTAURANT

BY BRIDGET HEOS  ILLUSTRATED BY KATYA LONGHI

Amicus Illustrated is published by Amicus
P.O. Box 1329, Mankato, MN 56002
www.amicuspublishing.us

Library of Congress Cataloging-in-Publication Data
Heos, Bridget, author.
 Manners at a restaurant / by Bridget Heos ;
Illustrated by Katya Longhi.
     pages cm. – (Monstrous manners)
 Summary: "A young monster with no manners
goes out to eat with a human family and learns
the manners he should use at a restaurant"–
Provided by publisher.
 ISBN 978-1-60753-744-1 (library binding)
 ISBN 978-1-60753-844-8 (ebook)
1. Table etiquette–Juvenile literature. I. Longhi,
Katya, illustrator. II. Title.
 BJ2041.H46 2016
 395.5'4–dc23   2014036516

Editor: Rebecca Glaser
Designer: Kathleen Petelinsek

Printed in the United States of America at
Corporate Graphics in North Mankato, Minnesota.

10 9 8 7 6 5 4 3 2 1

ABOUT THE AUTHOR

Bridget Heos is the author of more than
70 books for children including *Mustache
Baby* and *Mustache Baby Meets His Match*.
Her favorite manners are holding the door
for others and jumping up to help. You can
find out more about her, if you please, at
www.authorbridgetheos.com.

ABOUT THE ILLUSTRATOR

Katya Longhi was born in southern Italy.
She studied illustration at the Nemo
NT Academy of Digital Arts in Florence.
She loves to create dream worlds with
horses, flying dogs, and princesses in
her illustrations. She currently lives in
northern Italy with her Prince Charming.

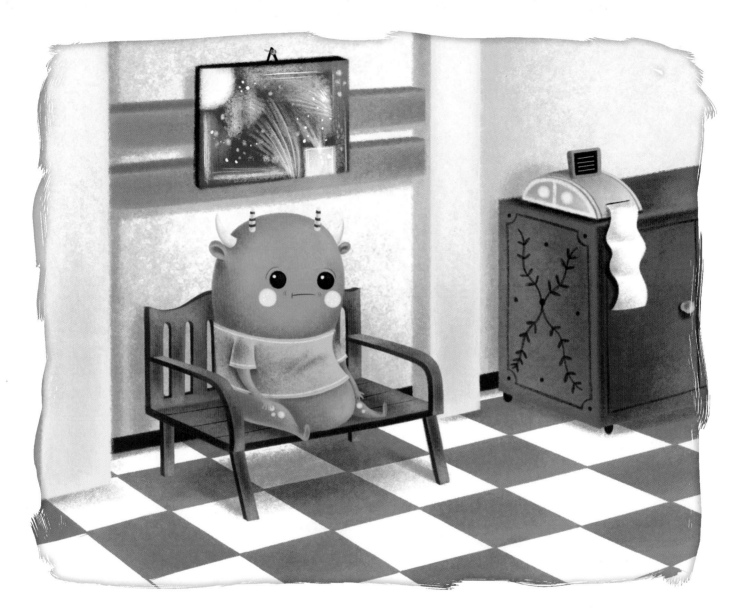

Hello, Monster. I see you're in time out for having bad manners. Don't worry, I'll show you how to have good manners at a restaurant.

Let's start over. What is the polite way to walk inside?
Ouch! No, no, Monster. Hold the door for others.

See, it was nice to help the marching band, Monster. And don't forget to take off your hats, everyone.

Now we wait to be seated.
Monster? Monster! Where did
you go?

7

You can't seat yourself unless there is a sign that says so!

Wait for the hostess to seat you. Here's our table.

Wait for the server to take your drink order. Now is NOT a
good time to practice drums. You'll bother the other diners.

When it is your turn to order, speak clearly and say please. They do not have spider juice, Monster. Order from the menu. How about lemonade?

Drink politely. No blowing bubbles. No slurping.

And obviously no sticking straws up your nose!

It's time to order dinner. Good job saying please,
Monster. But it's not time for dessert yet!

And it's never a good time to throw
a fit! Take a deep breath. Try again.

15

Monster, this isn't a playground! I know it's hard
to wait for your food. But you must stay seated.

And it's not a napping place, either.
Let's play tic-tac-toe while we wait.

THANK YOU.

Don't say bad things about other people's food. Let them enjoy it and you enjoy yours. Wait. Before you eat, put your napkin on your lap.

Don't forget to use your silverware to eat. Not like that! Use your fork and knife.

When you finish, wait for the server to take your plate. I know, there's a lot of waiting. But some things are worth the wait!

21

Hey, you're not a monster after all! You're my little brother.
Good job replacing your monstrous manners with good ones, Nick!

GOOD MANNERS WHEN EATING OUT

1. Hold the door for others.
2. Take off your hat inside.
3. Wait to be seated.
4. Be respectful of other diners. Don't be too loud. Don't run around. You could knock down a server carrying food.
5. Speak clearly and say "please" when ordering.
6. Wait patiently.
7. Don't slurp or blow bubbles in your drink.
8. Put your napkin on your lap.
9. Use your silverware to eat, but don't play with the silverware.
10. Don't criticize other people's food.

READ MORE

Ingalls, Ann. *Good Table Manners*. Mankato, Minn.: The Child's World, 2013.

Keller, Laurie. *Do Unto Otters: a Book About Manners*. New York: Henry Holt, 2007.

Marsico, Katie and John Haslam. *Good Manners in a Restaurant*. Edina, Minn.: Magic Wagon, 2009.

McGuirk, Leslie and Alex VonBidder. *Wiggins Learns His Manners at the Four Seasons Restaurant*. Somerville, Mass.: Candlewick Press, 2009.

Smith, Siân. *Manners at the Table*. Chicago: Heineman Library, 2013.

WEBSITES

Can You Teach My Alligator Manners?
disneyjunior.com/can-you-teach-my-alligator-manners
Watch videos and do activities to learn about manners in all different places, including restaurants, school, and more.

Learn about Manners: Crafts and Activities for Kids
www.dltk-kids.com/crafts/miscellaneous/manners.htm
Try these songs, crafts, and coloring pages to learn and practice good manners.

Top Table Manners for Kids
www.emilypost.com/home-and-family-life/children-and-teens/408-top-table-manners-for-kids
Learn more about table manners from expert Emily Post.